Bible For Dummies: Bible Journaling Made Easy

Speedy Publishing LLC
40 E. Main St. #1156
Newark, DE 19711

www.speedypublishing.com

Copyright 2015
9781681275727
First Printed January 12, 2015

This Book Belongs To:

____

Today I'm grateful for:

Prayer requests:

Self Improvement:

____

Principles to Apply:

Actions to Take:

Today I'm grateful for:

Prayer requests:

Self Improvement:

Principles to Apply:

Actions to Take:

Today I'm grateful for:

Prayer requests:

Self Improvement:

Principles to Apply:

Actions to Take:

Today I'm grateful for:

Prayer requests:

Self Improvement:

Principles to Apply:

Actions to Take:

Today I'm grateful for:

Prayer requests:

Self Improvement:

Principles to Apply:

Actions to Take:

Today I'm grateful for:

Prayer requests:

Self Improvement:

Principles to Apply:

Actions to Take:

Today I'm grateful for:

Prayer requests:

Self Improvement:

Principles to Apply:

Actions to Take:

Today I'm grateful for:

Prayer requests:

Self Improvement:

Principles to Apply:

Actions to Take:

Today I'm grateful for:

Prayer requests:

Self Improvement:

Principles to Apply:

Actions to Take:

Today I'm grateful for:

Prayer requests:

Self Improvement:

Principles to Apply:

Actions to Take:

Today I'm grateful for:

Prayer requests:

Self Improvement:

Principles to Apply:

Actions to Take:

Today I'm grateful for:

Prayer requests:

Self Improvement:

Principles to Apply:

Actions to Take:

Today I'm grateful for:

Prayer requests:

Self Improvement:

Principles to Apply:

Actions to Take:

Today I'm grateful for:

Prayer requests:

Self Improvement:

Principles to Apply:

Actions to Take:

Today I'm grateful for:

Prayer requests:

Self Improvement:

Principles to Apply:

Actions to Take:

Today I'm grateful for:

Prayer requests:

Self Improvement:

Principles to Apply:

Actions to Take:

Today I'm grateful for:

Prayer requests:

Self Improvement:

Principles to Apply:

Actions to Take:

Today I'm grateful for:

Prayer requests:

Self Improvement:

Principles to Apply:

Actions to Take:

Today I'm grateful for:

Prayer requests:

Self Improvement:

Principles to Apply:

Actions to Take:

Today I'm grateful for:

Prayer requests:

Self Improvement:

Principles to Apply:

Actions to Take:

Today I'm grateful for:

Prayer requests:

Self Improvement:

Principles to Apply:

Actions to Take:

Today I'm grateful for:

Prayer requests:

Self Improvement:

Principles to Apply:

Actions to Take:

Today I'm grateful for:

Prayer requests:

Self Improvement:

Principles to Apply:

Actions to Take: